Community Regeneration and the Local Church

Samuel Wells

Priest-in-Charge of St Mark's, Newnham, Cambridge

GROVE BOOKS LIMITED
RIDLEY HALL RD   CAMBRIDGE   CB3 9HU

Contents

The Cover Illustration is by Peter Ashton

First Impression June 2003
ISSN 0144-171X
ISBN 1 85174 532 7

Estate Regeneration in National Context

Some clergy live in deprived areas because they understand that these are the people with whom Jesus chose to spend most of his time, and they simply want to be where Jesus is.

Other clergy believe Jesus provides an answer to most or all of the problems of people in deprived areas, and they see living in such areas as bringing Jesus to those who need him most. The first kind can become Eeyores—weary but phlegmatic. The second kind can become Tiggers—eager but easily hurt. I came as the new incumbent to St Elizabeth's in Norwich in April 1997 as one of the first kind. It was a tiny congregation—around 15 adults and 7 (unrelated) children. Some wanted me to bring revival. Others wanted me to give them a break. I wanted them to show me God.

This booklet tells the story of how another kind of salvation invaded us. Sometimes it felt like a heresy; sometimes it felt like the real thing. Either way, when someone says 'If money weren't a problem, what would your dream community be like?' one cannot ignore it. That is what started to happen in the autumn of 1998.

This booklet tells the story of how another kind of salvation invaded us

When New Labour came to power in May 1997, it quickly set up the Social Exclusion Unit, with permission to use consultation and imagination to address the more intractable issues of poverty and marginalization in British society.

Exclusion is not just a matter of justice. It is a major concern of the Exchequer, for welfare far outstrips any other single item on the Chancellor's budget. Integrate the disaffected and isolated with the mainstream of training and employment—and crime, health, and education statistics will obligingly fall into a more agreeable rhythm. That is the logic.

Those who had been seeking to address these issues over many years, through the civil service, through statutory agencies such as social services, and through the voluntary sector, faced the new regime with mixed feelings. For some, it felt like a new golden era, with serious money at last heading for the people who needed it most. For others, perhaps those in the game a long time, there was a sense that experienced practitioners would get all the blame for the 'failed ideas of the past,' while New Labour would take the credit for any bright new proposals that might emerge.

The Conservatives had recognized that urban deprivation carried with it issues that neither central nor local government could resolve alone. There was increasing interest in attracting the private sector into the conversation, recognizing that businesses employ a great number of people, and their ethos and influence stretch well beyond working hours. As the Tories sought to reduce the percentage of national wealth spent on the various branches of government, the voluntary sector ceased to be the poor relation, and was rehabilitated as a vital component of social policy toward the most excluded communities. Experience proved that too many small initiatives brought confusion and weariness, so funds were funnelled into one pot, known as the Single Regeneration Budget. But one group, it seemed, had never been involved or consulted in the process of neighbourhood regeneration: the residents themselves.

What if such initiative could be turned into social capital?

Rather than see marginalized communities as dens of vice —human energy turned towards malicious purposes—a more positive understanding sees such neighbourhoods as sources of remarkable resourcefulness, of people who, though they have seldom perhaps known what it means to thrive, have nonetheless managed to survive on low incomes, often with unsettled families and without regular forms of emotional or financial security and stability. What if such initiative could be turned into social capital, and issues that had defeated bureaucrats be taken on by local people themselves?

The Dream

Give a community a huge sum of money—say £40 million—over a long period—say 10 years. Let them organize themselves, decide what they see as the problems that needed addressing, plan how they want to spend the money, and devise a process for identifying, shaping, monitoring and evaluating the various projects they had initiated to bring about this regeneration. What a thought! It would need to start with an existing, recognized body through whose accounts the Government could confidently pass its money. It would need support from the private, statutory and voluntary sectors in the wider community around the estate in question. It would need supervision from the regional Government office, to prevent any of the 'same old faces' in local government and elsewhere hijacking the process. It would be a significant social experiment.

If it worked, it would provide a stream of new ideas, tried and tested in deprived neighbourhoods, and proven to succeed where countless solutions imposed from outside had failed. It would shape social policy for the next generation, bending statutory investment towards methods that local people had faith in, and thus creating a forum in which local people could have a major say in how their neighbourhood was managed. And it would grow a whole generation of community leaders, people who had never before had the confidence or the opportunity to run institutions that contributed to the well-being of their community, who had perhaps experienced discrimination because of their postcode or personal background, but who had now learned to find their way around the labyrinth of organizational practice and to live with the cauldron of local politics—role models for their families and neighbours for years to come. That would indeed be regeneration—and good value for money.

If it worked, it would shape social policy for the next generation

This is the wager that New Labour made in launching its programme of community-led regeneration in 1998. There are currently 39 New Deal for Communities schemes running across England, in deprived estates with around 4,000 houses in each. So far this has remained a quiet revolution. It has gone largely unnoticed in Middle England, with its heart on the left and its wallet on the right. It has stayed out of election broadcasts and political point-scoring. But for the local church, as I shall now describe, this revolution poses some genuine challenges, and requires some genuine choices.

2

Context

Norwich is generally regarded as a prosperous city. Its medieval centre, peppered with churches and pubs, is a favourite with tourists and shoppers. Few think of the city in terms of urban deprivation.

In the 1930s the City Council embarked on a major programme of slum clearance. Among other projects, the North Earlham estate was built on a green field site, two miles to the west of the city centre. It became notorious. It gained the popular name 'the Larkman' from the pub where, it was widely supposed, crimes were plotted and fights began. In addition to those who had left poverty in the city came those driven from agricultural work by mechanization and, later, members of the travelling community. The comparatively spacious houses meant it was always a place for large, and often extended, families. Twenty years after gaining the right to buy their homes, only 10% of residents have done so, so the estate still looks and feels uniform in character. 3,000 people live on the estate, and in 1999 half of the households lived on less than £7,500 a year.

> *3,000 people live on the estate, and in 1999 half of the households lived on less than £7500 a year*

A church hall, known as St Elizabeth's, was built in the centre of the estate in 1938. The faithful congregation had a strong record of work with children, but the building was always vulnerable to vandalism. A new church, multi-purpose in style, was built in 1991. What should have been a wonderful opportunity became a catastrophe. Vocal members of the community wondered why the money could not have been spent on something residents genuinely wanted—and if it had to be a church, why not a proper one? The congregation's spirituality was largely one that looked for tangible signs of ordered grace. Having made the old hall look very much like a church, they now had a real church that would resist all efforts to make it look normal. Once the new church opened, the residents' dismay gradually ebbed away into indifference, while the congregation's bewilderment flowed toward embarrassment. Meanwhile the local young people's mischievous subversion of the building process grew out of hand and turned to anger. The unofficial adventure playground that was the building site had become a solid, apparently exclusive, edifice. A five-year campaign of sometimes violent intimidation ensued.

When I came to be vicar in April 1997 I sensed three issues of equal importance. Most urgent was to heal the relationship with the young people. A three-year youth project addressed this by engaging many young people in a host of activities, initially inside the building and eventually elsewhere. The building ceased to be seen as an alien space capsule. Next was to increase the congregation's self-esteem, towards their worship and towards their building. Gradually a style of worship emerged appropriate to faith and context. In 2000 a prayer room was refurbished and enhanced by

No wonder so few people came to church: it would mean leaving one family and joining another

two four-foot-square stained glass windows—a defining moment for a new era. The third issue was to form appropriate partnerships with people and organizations in the neighbourhood. Though big-hearted and faithful, the numerically small and vulnerable congregation were not well-placed to do this. So I took to attending three or four community meetings each month, to get to know what and who made the neighbourhood tick. What I found was a variety of formal and informal groups, the most vibrant of which operated like extended families—which some of them in fact were. No wonder so few people came to church; it would mean leaving one family and joining another.

Regeneration in Four Phases

1. Sept 1998–March 1999
In September 1998 Norwich City Council learned that Norwich was to have one of the 17 Pathfinder New Deal for Communities programmes. They gathered together a group of statutory and voluntary grandees and settled on North Earlham as the appropriate area. Because it was not quite big enough to qualify, they added on the small Marlpit estate to the north. Local statutory and voluntary representatives were invited to attend a Westminster briefing day. 25 people, including me, went, and this 'bus' became a significant identity-forming moment for a group of people who had seldom previously seen themselves as fighting a common cause.

Nothing forms identity quite like a common enemy, and the City Council quickly emerged as a suitable candidate. Most residents could tell a story of mistreatment by their common landlord, and all sensed a lingering mistrust from the city as a whole. So when the officer responsible hired a local school hall and set out a presentation that seemed to tell, rather than ask, the residents what the broad themes of the programme would be, the lingering resentments of many years flared into a joint moment of fury.

The residents decided that this was their scheme and no one was going to take it from them. A meeting was arranged at the church at which the Leader of the Council was taken to task. Four residents, again including me, went to the next meeting of the grandees and told them that from now on things would lie in the residents' hands. Nine people, two from formal voluntary agencies and six residents, formed a core group to handle the process until a legitimate board could be elected. I chaired the group, and the meetings took place at the church. The City Council loaned a part-time project manager, some local people were hired to set up an office (in a school) and distribute publicity, and a process of consultation began. Trust was at a minimum, and tempers were short.

Two public meetings took place in the middle school in March 1999, attended by 200 people. Both teetered on the edge of chaos, but out of them emerged a board of 31 people, with representatives of statutory and voluntary agencies, business, and over 20 residents, one of whom became the chair. It was not tidy—but it was a start.

2. March 1999–April 2000
Four issues dominated the subsequent twelve months: building authority and trust, within the organization and without; establishing an executive structure and employing people in its key roles; developing procedures that guaranteed progress in such areas; and developing a policy for spending the vast sum of money.

Few moments crystallized the process as much as the appointment of the project manager. If a person were appointed from outside the community, would that be saying local people did not know what was best for their community? If the person were paid a large salary, what would that say to people who were struggling to make ends meet on a fifth of that sum? Should the new organization be run like a local authority, like a business, or like a project in the developing world? Could anyone bridge the culture of the neighbourhood and that of the 'suits' in the public agencies and private sector? An extensive appointment process ensued, and a consensus emerged around one candidate, from an armed forces and business background. It proved a sound appointment. But filling the other posts was another story, and getting the right balance of skill, potential and experience, employing local people and 'outsiders,' was a very delicate matter.

Few moments crystallized the process as much as the appointment of the project manager

The lack of authority and trust bedevilled the process. Some hearts and minds adapted well to the need for urgency and visible results; others responded better to the time-consuming practices of taking minutes, establishing standing orders, consulting widely, and forming lasting partnerships. Few enjoyed both. At times everyone felt and behaved like a victim of exclusion. Local people, excluded and patronized and undervalued over many years, were highly sensitive to any suggestion that they were not 'good enough' to handle money, take decisions, govern a process or hold executive roles. Others, who felt they had a stake in the community, but due to living on the wrong side of the road or not shouting loud enough (sometimes literally) to make their voices heard, felt they were being ignored. And so-called 'agencies,' professionals who had experience and skills and commitment to offer, sometimes felt treated as leeches because they seemed to grow in number as soon as a large Government-funded project appeared.

At times everyone felt and behaved like a victim of exclusion

Somehow the project manager put together a hundred-page Delivery Plan. Focus groups, covering the six key areas of Education, Employment, Health, Community Safety, Drugs, and Sports/Arts/Leisure, met and combined local experience of problems with local government statistics, and local ideas and initiatives with reports and schemes being tried elsewhere. Residents went on fact-finding missions to other regeneration schemes, and a survey of a third of local houses established what those who lived in the neighbourhood saw as the priorities.

There emerged four kinds of proposals.

a   The heart of the Delivery Plan lay in affirming, resourcing, strengthening and expanding the variety of voluntary organizations that already existed in the neighbourhood. Ideas that had long existed in local people's imaginations, or run on a shoestring, aimed to become substantial concerns. A 'schoolwatch' security service made a bid to become a community wardens scheme. A dance-and-football youth group made a bid to expand into a substantial youth organization. A carnival club made a bid to transform from making costumes for the annual Lord Mayor's procession to offering a year-round craft and leisure activity.

b   Meanwhile, a second string of proposals gave city-wide voluntary organizations an opportunity to develop targeted programmes in the local community. The YMCA aimed to place pastoral care workers in the schools. Two people who had experience of the

Women's Refuge made a bid to establish an organization helping people develop family skills. The Theatre Royal looked to target toward the regeneration area a talent school for performing arts. A support network for small businesses set up training sessions in the neighbourhood.

c A third set of proposals came from the bright ideas unearthed by the community survey. Community radio, community transport, community support workers—practical schemes to address immediate needs.

d Finally there were the large-scale major projects for long-term change. An employment agency was set up. Much work went into a coordinated childcare strategy, to benefit children, enable parents to access work and training, to provide local employment, and, in time, to offer a potential local business opportunity to service the rest of the city, turning the city's burden into a carrier of the city's burdens. Much attention focused on the flagship project, the purchase of a former secondary school site, and its redevelopment for business and housing purposes, thus providing an income stream for sustainable leisure facilities.

3. April 2000–June 2002

There was great satisfaction when in April 2000 the Government announced that £35.6 million had been awarded to the Norwich New Deal for Communities Scheme. The period that followed required great patience on all sides, as they set about translating organizations oriented to gaining funding into structures capable of delivering results. The issues that dominated the second period had not gone away, and there were new expectations and frustrations at every turn. Constant tension lay between the short-term and the long-term aspirations of the process. These were manifested in three specific ways.

a One lay within the projects themselves. The transition from a hand-to-mouth family structure to an institutional model with clear roles and accountabilities was a painful one for some organizations, and vital energy was burnt off in exasperation. Meanwhile the appraisal, approval, monitoring and quality assurance structures of the overall organization were in their infancy. The Government, with a rhetoric of unleashing ideas but an instinct to control expenditure, seemed to be making up the rules as it went along. The air felt thick with broken promises, reinvented wheels and red tape. Yet if these projects were to be launched on a sound footing, careful attention to detail was required. Those offering this attention to detail seemed suspiciously like the same old faces against whom so much anger had been expressed at the start of the process.

b   A number of factors inhibited the relationship between NDC Norwich and the local authorities—the abrasive style of the residents, the perception that the area now had plenty of its own money, and the slowness to grasp the novelty of the new context. For example, the people involved in NDC could not see why deprived areas were not being specifically targeted for extra investment rather than get the same blanket resourcing as more affluent areas.

c   The third tension lay in the formation of a new institution. If the organization was ever to stand on its own feet (the City Council were still, after all, the bankers, and therefore the employers of the core staff), it needed to become a legal entity. Yet the need to press ahead with projects and develop a legal structure inhibited the equally urgent need for legitimate authority. There had only, after all, been a kangaroo election at a chaotic public meeting. After much heart-searching, the board decided to set aside its concerns over its own legitimacy, and in October 2000 it turned itself into a company limited by guarantee—the North Earlham, Larkman and Marlpit Development Trust. There were 12 resident directors, and 11 other directors from the private, statutory and voluntary sectors. It took another 18 months before elections could be held.

4. June 2002 onwards

Over the two years from the submission of the Delivery Plan most of the frustrations were overcome. Projects did start; partnerships and trust did grow; and community elections to the Board of Directors were held in the spring of 2002. By June 2002 the NELM Development Trust had everything it needed to regenerate its community. It had the will of local people. It had a structure for delivery. It had ideas, and a strategy for their implementation. It had a structure to facilitate the process. It had partnerships between local people and a variety of organizations and agencies. It had an elected board of directors who knew they carried the confidence of the local community. It had plenty of money. It had solicitors and accountants and other professional support. It had a track record of small but generally successful projects over the previous two years. And it had an increasing number of local people who had benefited in some way from involvement in the process and had gained experience, confidence or encouragement to make a positive and significant contribution to their families, their neighbourhood, and wider society.

I chose this moment to stand down from the board of directors. Over the previous four years I had held a number of formal roles. I had at times chaired the main board, the executive committee, and the policy committee. I had continued to be vice-chair of the board, chair of the childcare initiative, and a member of the employment focus group. I participated in a pattern of training, networking, and representing the organization locally and nationally. In general I had concentrated on strategic issues like the shape of the legal entity, the internal functioning of the organization and ways of anticipating crises and pitfalls. I now felt that I had more to offer the neighbourhood as a vicar than as a development worker. It was time to assess the social, theological and pastoral significance of this remarkable process.

It was time to assess the social, theological and pastoral significance of this remarkable process

The Challenge of Regeneration: What the Church Can Learn

3

Regeneration means rebirth. It means being born again.

Put like that, it is easy to see that New Deal for Communities, and similar schemes, are offering a kind of salvation. How does it compare with the salvation of which the church speaks?

Jesus set about regeneration. He was a resident of a deprived area. The Holy Land was a land deprived of self-government, liberty, and justice—and Galilee was second-class in the Holy Land of its day. At his baptism, the voice from heaven declared that Jesus was the one through whom God would bring regeneration. Jesus began his programme of regeneration by taking time out (40 days) to consider. During this time he rejected the temptations of the instant, the dramatic and the short-term. He then called a committed group of 12 people to change society from within. Together, they made themselves familiar with the needs and hopes of all the people in the regeneration area (Israel), especially the most needy, and filled their hearts with the hope of redemption. He challenged the people who were making the nation's oppression worse, those who withheld resources from the poor and those who sought their own well-being without regard to God's justice and mercy. He embodied what he propounded, and took opportunities to show people how they could live in the new era that was breaking in (the kingdom of God). He paused to address particular crises, especially when they had symbolic significance, and when they demonstrated his underlying purpose (miracles), even when doing so seemed to break traditional practice. All this time he was teaching and training his key partners so that they might later be able to follow in his steps. He taught and showed them what it meant to depend utterly on God and prepare for the time of trial. After his ascension the disciples were empowered by his Holy Spirit to do remarkable things like him. They fully used the gifts they had been given, and in the process discovered gifts they never knew they had. Christ gave his followers a Great Commission—to continue his work in his authority. Some while later, they were clothed with the power to carry this commission through.

> *It is easy to see that New Deal for Communities is offering a kind of salvation*

Then and Now

Compare this with the story of regeneration I have been describing. The local people most closely involved in the process have a role very much like that of the disciples in the gospel story. They live in a deprived area. They become well informed of the perspectives of the entire neighbourhood, for example through regular large-participation surveys. They stay close to the poorest, challenging those (whether employers, consumers, service providers or unruly neighbours) whose practice exacerbates the problem. And they sometimes address extreme cases of need rapidly without using a complex instrument of authority. Meanwhile they seek encouragement, training and formation to grow into the leadership of the neighbourhood long after the injection of government funding has passed.

Jesus drew his followers from these kinds of people. They sometimes fail, and the burden of personal failure is the greater for the knowledge that it brings discredit on the regeneration process as a whole. But most of the people involved in the process can look back on their involvement with considerable pride. Those who have not stayed with the institutional aspect of regeneration have gone on to run some of the projects, to enter local politics, or to benefit their community in some other way. The lasting benefits of such regeneration will depend on these people, just as the early church depended on the disciples. How many churches can honestly say they are as close as this to local needs and concerns, and as committed as this to local empowerment?

The lasting benefits of such regeneration will depend on these people

If the community-led regeneration process finds analogies in the gospels, it does also in the Acts of the Apostles. The members of the community who lead the regeneration process are very much like a church in significant ways. There is a commitment to meeting regularly. There is a regular pattern to which these meetings generally conform. There is a constant retelling of the story by which the development trust came to be formed, and the values and common purpose that underlie it. The initial sense of grievance is gradually displaced by the increasing record of finding solutions through new partnerships. There is a commitment to, and an increasingly formalized process of, the cordial resolution of differences. There is a strong desire to spread the good news, and to include the most marginalized members of the community in the deliberations and results. There is a constant determination to point local residents in the direction of hope. Most impressively, there is an ability to tolerate hurt, anger, abuse and humiliation, to seek to understand, to work beyond and even forgive, that would put many, perhaps most, churches to shame.

Living in the Present Tense

The greatest strength of the regeneration process has been to live in the present tense. How the estate came to have such a terrible reputation, who is to blame for the underlying problems of the community, and indeed what those underlying problems genuinely are—these questions are seldom discussed. Attention instead rests on how local people can be empowered to become artisans of their own destiny. This assumes that they are capable of doing so. It assumes that the community already has within it most or all of what it needs to be everything it can be. And it assumes that the community has a distinct sense of what its own thriving means; in other words, it aspires to be what only it can be—not to cast its eyes covetously to other communities and wonder if it can have what they have.

Local people can be empowered to become artisans of their own destiny

Few churches can tell such a positive story. Many have such a dominant notion of sin that they struggle to articulate and believe in the underlying goodness of God's creation. Many have such an overwhelming sense of the priority of God's grace that they struggle to see the validity of helping people find their own solutions to their own problems. Many have such a profound sense of the otherness of God's coming kingdom that they miss the glory of God in people endeavouring collaboratively to become more fully alive. Some of the most painful lessons in the New Deal for Communities process have been those learned by professionals who slowly realized that their experience and expertise sometimes not only failed to solve the problem, but often made the problem worse and in some cases *were* the problem. Many churches, even in deprived communities, share that professional mindset. How many churches 'carry' the passive sabotage of those who did not really agree in the first place but had never been encouraged to join the conversation, instead assuming that their thoughts did not matter, their experience was irrelevant and their educational frustrations made them unworthy? It is easy to see how in the 'them and us' of the regeneration process, many churches behave like and thus become the 'them.'

In the 'them and us' of the process, many churches behave like and thus become the 'them'

Consumer Politics

But perhaps the most important prophetic statement of the community-led regeneration process to church and world in our time is its understanding of politics. Middle England has developed a consumer view of politics. This largely passive view assumes politics is largely about the efficient management of statutory services. This is why the great public debates surround what people get for their money—particularly in terms of health, education, and safe neighbourhoods. Politicians are regarded as substandard shop assistants, finding endless excuses for poor service, and probably on the take in some way. The cynicism towards politicians corresponds with the public's low view of their importance. Who would want such an uninspiring and insecure job unless there was something in it for them? Underlying this view is a bland realism, which recognizes that people are selfish and thus that politics is about the fair distribution of scarce (or at least limited) resources.

The community-led regeneration view of politics is different. Politics is not just a tiresome consequence of human shortcomings, it is an ongoing conversation about how to bring out and empower the ocean of different gifts and talents in a community. It is not about the limited money in people's pockets, it is about the limitless potential in their hearts and minds and souls and bodies. It is about how to engage all the energy that is about, and how to discern and embody that which constitutes the good life. It may not always be happy, beautiful, or rich, but if a community can express such a notion of politics, it can experience a goodness that other communities, with their impoverished politics, can only envy.

How to bring out and empower the ocean of different gifts and talents in a community

And these 'other communities' frequently include churches. Churches often pick up from their surrounding culture a view of politics that sees tiresome negotiations over resources as one of many consequences of the Fall. This is reflected, for many Church of England churches, in a very negative perception of the parish share system and the synodical structure of the church. By contrast the people involved in community-led regeneration know that the decisions taken at meetings are only a small part of the overall process. They understand that true politics is a lengthy deliberation over the good, with helpful detours into the discernment of the right, the true and the beautiful. This is a view of politics that realizes that such debate is an integral part of the nature and purpose of human beings, even before the Fall. It has much to teach the church.

The Challenge of Regeneration: What the Church Can Offer

4

I have suggested that the greatest strength of the regeneration process of which I have been a part is to live in the present tense.

This is a tremendous asset, because it avoids the debilitating cynicism of those who have seen previous schemes fail, and it allays the nagging fear of those who have no experience of the future being better than the past. But the price of living in the present tense is relative silence on the questions that lie behind regeneration. Why is this neighbourhood poor? Whose fault is it? What would this community be like if it was the best that it could be? Who would gain and who would lose if it changed?

The congregation and building of a church are a witness that there is more to life than this present moment

The congregation and building of a church in a local community are a witness that there is more to life than this present moment. They are a statement that the world and its inhabitants came from somewhere, are going somewhere, and that events that happened at a particular time and place—in Palestine 2,000 years ago—have a vital significance for shaping and disclosing the truth about us and the world.

The Story the Church Tells

Where Does the Story Begin?
The church's story begins with God. For Christians, the history of the world is the unfolding story of God's revelation of his own character through his interaction with his creation.

The local church seeks to imitate a God who is personal. It will therefore emphasize renewed people rather than new buildings. It will aspire not to abstract benefits such as health and peace but to personal growth in inner confidence and technical proficiency. It is important that regeneration aspires to a dynamic outcome, not a static one. The very word 'estate' implies a static model of society. But the aim of regeneration should be a society that is open to creative change over time and organic change within space. The Christian notion of God is more a dance than a statue.

Dynamic personality must mean relationship. The dance of God is a dynamic relationship between the persons of Father, Son and Holy Spirit. Because modern government increasingly depends on economic notions of flourishing, and modern economic notions of flourishing rest on an understanding of the autonomous individual, there will invariably be a tension between the local church's understanding of regeneration based on restored relationship, and the government's commitment to regeneration based on empowered independence.

The Christian notion of God is more a dance than a statue

This commitment to understanding the Trinity as relationship between persons lends itself to the notion of Trinity as community. This leads the local church to aspire to a regeneration process that values the worth and contribution of every single member of the neighbourhood. Not only should every person have the chance to offer every aspect of themselves, but the process is diminished unless each respective aspect is fully received and enjoyed and allowed to grow and develop.

The bonds of interdependent indwelling community in the Trinity are bonds of mutual self-emptying love. The self-giving which is revealed in God's ways with the world is embodied in the relations of the persons of the Trinity with one another. The heart of Christian faith is the belief that this passionate and compassionate love for the other is the strongest force in the universe, stronger than any rival. The risk taken by the Christian in believing this is as nothing compared with the risk taken by God in demonstrating it. The local church aspires to embody this self-emptying love in its relationships within the fellowship and in its witness and service in the neighbourhood. Of the regeneration process, it expects that the goal of the process will be a community in which such love can grow. Both ends and means will include the building of trust, the maintenance of stability, the establishment of authority, the centrality of relationship and cooperation rather than property and possession, the value placed on rearing children, and the respect and encouragement offered to the most dependent and vulnerable people and their carers.

The Christian faith in God focuses on a mystery and a truth. The mystery is why God took upon himself the trouble of entering into relationship with such an unsteady and faithless partner as his creation, particularly its human dimension, has proved to be. Even greater than this mystery is the truth that he did make that choice, that he did elect in an act of grace to make a people and make himself known to them, and to maintain that relationship despite its terrible cost. Indeed he shaped his very being to make those things possible and enact them. If the local church participates in urban regeneration, it must seek to reflect the wonder and challenge of this gracious election. In all the talk of education and opportunity, it must not neglect the deeper qualities of imagination and wonder. Unless imagination and wonder have space and time to grow, it will not be conceivable that such a God could exist. In all the talk of choice the local church must remember and celebrate that the decisive choice was God's choice never to exist unless for his beloved

The goal of regeneration is good people, pouring out their lives in the service of one another

creation, and to shape his life for our salvation. If choice is to be prized so highly, there must be opportunity for people to have not just independence, the ability to choose, but also freedom, the ability to make good choices. The local church should continue to offer examples that demonstrate that the goal of regeneration is not good buildings, good government, good services, good jobs, or good incomes—important as each of these are—but good people, pouring out their lives in the service of one another.

Where is the Story Going?

Though the most pressing issues in regeneration concern the style of involvement in the plans and delivery bodies themselves, perhaps the most significant underlying questions are eschatological. What kind of a society do we want to live in? One like we used to have? One like they have today in the neighbouring suburb, a society of double-glazing, garden features and sparkling conservatories? Or a society that has never existed before? There is a contemporary reluctance to envisage the future. The rate of technological change, the demise of Marxist utopianism and liberal notions of perpetual progress, the complexity of contemporary life and its apparent domination by impersonal forces, together with fears of environmental apocalypse and the fragility of close relationships, all encourage people to think little beyond the present tense. Visions of hope tend to sound fundamentalist or utopian.

The local church strengthened by this faith will be content to be faithful rather than visibly effective

Hopes and fears surrounding the last things can be broadly separated into two kinds: those that focus on God's action; and those that are more concerned with human survival. The notion of God's activity clusters around images such as the return of Christ, the last judgment and the everlasting reign of God. These images relativize all human achievements and institutions. They ensure continuity between the salvation achieved in Christ and that fully revealed on the last day. They affirm God's vindication of those who have suffered unduly in earthly life, his reversal of oppression and mercy on the merciful. The local church strengthened by this faith will be content to be faithful rather than visibly effective. For it is better to fail in a cause (such as upholding the oppressed) which will finally succeed, than to succeed in a cause (such as ensuring every resident has a brand-new house) which will finally fail. It will be content to let God and future generations complete the work it has faithfully carried forward. It will be content to look back and simply realize it was on the winning side.

This attempt to reflect God's character summarized the local church's aspirations for its neighbourhood

The concern for human life in God, on the other hand, tends to dwell on the images of the resurrection of the body, heaven and hell. These combine personal urgency with cosmic scale. It is important for a local church to envision the dimensions of heaven, rather than just concentrate on who gets there. Human society in heaven is most appropriately conceived as a reflection of God's society in the Trinity. This attempt to reflect God's character summarizes the local church's aspirations for its neighbourhood.

Through reflection on where the story ends, a local church can formulate its aspirations for its neighbourhood, and develop a kind of social manifesto. It will hope that its community comes to imitate the character of God. It will imitate God by becoming a body of growing people—a people who live in a pattern of self-offering and other-receiving relationships, relationships that exhibit harmonious diversity. It will be a community at peace with its environment, and one that has a special heart for outcasts.

What is the Crucial Moment in the Story?

In my account of the process of community-led estate regeneration, I suggested that many of the features of the process had much in common with the way Jesus went about regeneration. The church is founded on faith in the centrality of Jesus Christ and the necessity and possibility of the salvation he brings. His revelation is the defining moment in history, and all other events and persons derive their meaning and significance in relation to it. Salvation means health and well being, now and forever; efforts at restoring and promoting health and well being in deprived communities must therefore have a bearing on Christian understandings of salvation. That is why the model of community-led regeneration is so significant for the local church.

Money can facilitate change— but it cannot transform reality

While the analogy of Jesus' approach to regeneration and the community-led approach is suggestive, it breaks down when one realizes that the role played by Jesus in the gospel story is taken in the community story by £35 million. Here the comparison fails, because no amount of money can do what Jesus did. Money can catalyse human action but money cannot die and be raised to life. Money can facilitate change—but it cannot transform reality.

While so much of Christ's model of salvation lies in his incarnation and ministry, so much also lies in his death and resurrection. The true society that Jesus proclaimed undermined the power-bases of the time. So much so, that when he began to speak of this true society within the walls of Jerusalem—in sight of the Jewish Temple and the Roman praetorium—he quickly became the victim of these powers. In doing so he accepted the personal cost of political confrontation. His vindication in the resurrection undermined the validity of all domination systems and showed that hope lies in the victim.

This is perhaps the most uncompromising dimension of the local church's understanding of regeneration. If it is to follow Christ's manner, it must recognize that regeneration does not come without suffering and sacrifice. In Christ's case the sufferers were not those who caused the problem but the one seeking a solution. The local church's faith is that God seeks the liberation of his people and will vindicate those who face the trial of political confrontation with faithfulness and dignity. This is seldom a popular gospel. After all, when the vital moment came, it was the oppressed themselves—those in the praetorium—who called for Jesus' death. The local church must continue to have the courage, on occasion, to call for a form of regeneration that is beyond and outside what many people in deprived communities may think they want. So many of the seeds for regeneration lie within the community itself. But not all.

The Church's Place in the Story

Where Does the Local Church Come in the Story?
The period between the salvation of God's creation in Christ and the consummation of God's purposes on the last day constitutes the theological space occupied by the church. The church's involvement in regeneration stems appropriately from its identification with the poor and heavy laden, those in whom it sees Christ's face and with whom it expects to share eternal life. This builds on the church's more general desire to see the flourishing of all God's people in body, mind and spirit—to see the glory of God in human beings fully alive. But the church also has a tradition of having a special vocation—based around repentance, forgiveness, worship, proclamation, holiness of life and a sense of coming judgment.

The gift of the Christian story is freedom. That freedom is a release from having to secure one's own salvation, freedom from having to make one's own and the world's story have a happy ending, freedom from having single-handedly to conquer the limitations and intimidating oppressors of life and to institute a commonwealth of love and peace all on one's own. It is a release from the burden of having to be effective, and an opportunity instead to be faithful.

Act justly, love mercy, walk humbly—there is no mention here of effectiveness

Faithfulness to the gospel is, however, seldom as attractive as participation in activity that brings quick and tangible results. Act justly, love mercy, walk humbly—there is no mention here of effectiveness. Churches in deprived areas can feel as depressed as the areas they serve. The temptation to set their vocation to one side for a taste of the intoxication of dramatic change can be hard to resist. The local church has to ask itself constantly whether economic regeneration is a distraction from true regeneration. Collaboration with those building a new Jerusalem may be collusion with a heresy. A healthy test of holiness may be the degree to which members and the church as a body remain close to the poorest, or get drawn into power games well beyond the estate itself. A church that stays close to the needs and concerns of the poor themselves cannot be far from the kingdom.

A church that stays close to the needs an concerns of the poor themselves cannot b far from the kingdon

And here lies the irony. A church that is close to the most vulnerable will often be too vulnerable to reach beyond immediate needs. I am proud of the fact that St Elizabeth's is not an 'aspirational' church—where the 'respectable working-classes' make a 'withdrawing-room' in which to worship God. St Elizabeth's is a stressed church, with the mental health fragility and precarious relationships and security that pervade the neighbourhood it serves. As vicar I often wondered whether participation in the regeneration process (on behalf of the congregation and community) was a distraction from the reality of particular people and fathomless problems.

What is the Local Church's Role in the Story?
If Christians fully understand that God does what only he can do, they are better able to do what only they can do. God alone has created. He alone, in Jesus, has died for the sake of his people. He alone has taken away the ultimate power of sin. He alone has empowered his people with the Holy Spirit, the living presence of Christ. And he alone will end the story when and how he sees fit. Because Christians trust that these things are safe with God, they

can value and get on with those things they have been entrusted to do. And if they respect one another's roles in the kingdom, they can release one another rather than tread on one another's toes.

God has given the local church a number of particular practices to shape and sustain and characterize its life. It may well think these unremarkable— unless it realizes that they constitute its most significant gift to a community-led regeneration process. Among these many, four stand out.

Baptism
Baptism is an acknowledgment that change is needed, a statement that change is possible, and a witness to the origin of that change. The community-led regeneration process needs a similar kind of honesty, a comparable kind of faith, and an analogous kind of courage. Baptism is all about change—and so is regeneration. Things will be different—there will be loss as well as gain; there must be public recognition of the need for change and public celebration of symbolic moments of change. Christians who know about change of heart can encourage a community that is experiencing it. The most moving experiences at St Elizabeth's have been the testimonies of those who have come for adult baptism. The most stirring experiences in the regeneration process have come when people have found sufficient acceptance and affirmation to be able to acknowledge that they perhaps have needed to change too.

Christians who know about change of heart can encourage a community that is experiencing it

Communion
At Communion, reconciliation is made, a story is recalled, gifts are presented, all are fed, and are then sent out with renewed purpose. Each of these practices offers important experience to a community seeking regeneration. Such a community needs to find ways to patch up quarrels, receive gifts, to share food and to reinvigorate tired minds and bodies. Communion is all about how God renews people through sharing food. Most of the important conversations in regeneration processes happen at meal tables rather than boardroom tables. Meanwhile, learning to eat well influences almost every aspect of regeneration—from healthy diets to more energy to fewer illnesses to fewer hyperactive children to table conversation and transferable culinary expertise.

Scripture
Reading Scripture is the way the church recognizes that others have sought to follow and serve God before. There is wisdom to be found, experience to be shared, truth to be learned. People there struggled with poverty and with

oppression long before we started to, and God showed his grace and glory as much through their failures as through their successes. So he will today. People's interest in Scripture parallels their interest in education. At the start of the regeneration process, few people felt that anything of value came out of books. Only experience—local experience—counted. Now experience has taught people that the wisdom of others matters. And that means books. The irony is that the congregation have gone the other way. Once they assumed that all wisdom came from books and the Book. Those who knew it best had control. Now they increasingly realize that their experience matters, and can be a 'book' to other communities.

Prayer

The community of faith wonder at God's choosing to include them in his story, are thankful for what seems like chance but they realize is providence, and offer all that is still beyond their strength, wit and power. Church meetings start with a prayer; regeneration meetings never do. For church regulars saying a prayer at the start of a meeting may have become a habit given scant consideration. But at a regeneration meeting, sensing something curiously missing which one has elsewhere taken for granted, one becomes slowly aware that this gathering is taking upon itself an enormous task—and is seeking to perform it in its own strength alone. How awesome is the sight! Habits of thankfulness and asking for help come easily to those used to prayer. They can benefit the regeneration process deeply. At times of tragedy and need—the death of a child, September 11th—board meetings began in silence. This is perhaps the least threatening, most humble contribution of the Christian—to find words to articulate common need.

This is perhaps the least threatening, most humble contribution of the Christian

What Can the Local Church do to Carry Out this Role?

If the role of the local church is to trust the practices God has given it and let him do the rest, what of the particular reference of these practices to an estate experiencing community-led regeneration?

If the local church trusts God to fulfil his role, and trusts that the practices he has given will prove liberating and sustaining, it will be set free to take a few risks. The whole community is being encouraged to take risks in regeneration, and the least the church can do is to do the same. For example, two key gifts a local church has to offer its community are time and space.

Churches in regeneration areas are much like all local organizations. Few people pay tax, many are single, some are on a pension, several are caring for troubled and needy relatives or neighbours. Money is short—but time and energy may be plentiful. They may feel that the time-consuming business of attending community meetings and putting together projects is time not spent worshipping and evangelizing. But if God has called them to do it, he will receive it as worship and find ways in which it puts feet on the gospel. Likewise the vicar or minister. To be closely involved in the process involves a sacrifice of time—perhaps a day or two a week, maybe even more. If this is truly God's call, it needs to be checked with others in neighbouring churches and with a bishop or similar authority. And then a partnership can be formed in which other churches or clergy support this gift of time and are rewarded in other ways.

Turning to space, a church in or near the heart of a regeneration area has a priceless gift of space. That space—the building—may prove a crucial, immediately available, low-cost meeting place for a crisis meeting or large gathering. If the congregation offer it in the spirit of service, God will receive it in the spirit of worship. Most of the early meetings in Norwich took place in the church. It was not everyone's choice, since smoking and vivid language were discouraged—but it was the only building available free and at short notice.

If the congregation offer it in the spirit of service, God will receive it in the spirit of worship

More subtly, the building offers remarkable potential for hospitality, for practical gestures of encouragement that affirm the goodness that already lies in the community. My congregation chose to convert some iron gates that had protected the front doors of the church into an inspiring wing sculpture to hang inside, symbolizing the new hope in the community. They also surrounded the area used for worship with photographs of notable characters, all of whom lived in the area around the church, but none of whom came to worship on a Sunday. A group of single mothers, who used the church for a weekly art class, identified the people concerned, shot, developed and mounted the photographs, and displayed them around the church. Thus the worshipping congregation were surrounded on a Sunday with those for whom they prayed. When the regeneration bid went to the Government in March 2000, there was a sudden search for photographs that expressed what was good about the community. The photographs on the church walls were ideal for the purpose, and were duly used. Thus had the local church's imaginative use of its own space helped the neighbourhood realize its human worth.

5

Key Choices

I found involvement in community-led regeneration to be an intense, sometimes exhilarating and sometimes draining experience.

There were constant choices to be made, risks to be taken, setbacks to be faced. The following seem, in retrospect, to have been the defining moments that marked the local church's relationship with the community-led process. Each is framed in terms of a question.

1 Should the local church be involved?

All my involvement in neighbourhood life before the regeneration process began was an effort to say 'God cares about what you care about, and your church wants to discover what God is doing here.' Involvement was therefore inevitable. Nonetheless there was a constant issue of whether church members were involved as 'church' or as 'resident.' Being a Christian was no serious problem, but being part of an interest group that many people suspected belonged outside the community invited considerable suspicion.

2 Should the involvement be proactive?

The vicar or minister is a community leader, like it or not. In late 1998, local people needed support in seizing control of the process. Giving that support entailed risks—stepping outside the boundaries of the 'vicar' role—but withholding it would have been much worse. Most of the time my role, and that of other church members, was that of a reconciler and behind-the-scenes diplomat. Any behind-the-scenes activity attracts suspicion. My visible role tended to be that of making public addresses or chairing testy meetings when no other resident was present or prepared to do so.

Any behind-the-scenes activity attracts suspicion

3 Who should be involved?

Those in a local congregation who do have an aptitude for institutional formation are probably already engaged in it—perhaps in local government.

These existing roles are not value-free. The ideal is that the vicar or minister can support others in engaging with the process; if not, others must support the vicar.

4 What kinds of involvement are possible?

I spent four years helping to lead the process—in a policy-making role at board level. But there are other roles on the board, there are many roles on the staff, on focus groups, on project boards, helping plan projects, volunteering for community groups and supporting all of the above. More important than *working for* the community is *working with* or, better, simply *being with* local people in their struggles. It is a demanding, complex world, and many regeneration schemes are far more labyrinthine, with a Venn diagram of complementary initiatives across an overlapping series of geographical areas. It is very hard to be taken seriously unless one gives it significant time and trouble.

More important than working for the community is simply being with the local people in their struggles

5 What will the local church NOT do in order to make the time available?

The heavy demands of the regeneration process forced me as vicar and in turn my congregation to re-examine its common life, mission and ministry. Most of the existing voluntary groups found that involvement in the regeneration process put their day-to-day operations under severe pressure. The church was no exception. A church that tries to do everything often reserves the right to do things badly. It also tends to see exhaustion as morally worthy. Reflection on these commonplaces of church life inclined us toward a more sustainable model of doing fewer things, but doing them well.

6 With what status is the church involved?

This is the question of incarnation. With what perception of itself does the local church participate in the process of regeneration? Is it an expert, with a long history, deep experience and perhaps the only resident professional person? Is it a vital institution, representing a voice that has a right to be heard? Is it a flexible asset, with useful influence at all levels well beyond the reach of most people in a deprived neighbourhood? Is it a voluntary organization, struggling to make ends meet like all the others? Is it a model of revolutionary organization, a prototype of a regeneration board? Or is it a handful of individuals with as much and as little to offer as any other local residents? Confusion on this matter can cause deep mistrust from all the other parties involved. The local church needs to avoid acting as a parent, expecting others to follow its example, and enjoy acting as a child, renouncing claims of status and learning and growing as it listens and contributes like everyone else.

7 Should the local church put in for a project?

This is a very significant decision. There can be an unseemly scuffle as local voluntary groups carve up the regeneration cake. If the church seeks to act in the general interest, this may be altruistic—or it may imply that the church believes it is above the messy business of funding and managing projects. Yet if the church does put in for specific projects, it may need to ask itself what distinguishes it from just another voluntary interest group. If the wider Church of England cannot continue to fund churches with small congregations in deprived communities, they may increasingly have to fund themselves via projects that may have little or no specific Christian identity. These are the risks of incarnation, and the choices are crucial.

8 What kind of project?

I resisted attempts to turn the church into a 'healthy living centre,' because I do not see Christianity as one form of therapy alongside others. I felt deeply uncomfortable about seeking funding for a church youth worker or similar because it might seem that my involvement had been self-seeking. And so the local church was one of the few voluntary groups that had no platform in the delivery plan. But the desire to be part of a project was still there. Eventually St Elizabeth's, reflecting on its experience of youth and children's work, perceived that the key to regeneration lay in the imagination of the child. The church put together a proposal, rooted in Christian spirituality but with an open and inclusive approach, that sought to give children the time, space and support to explore and develop their creative imaginations. The development trust found it had underspent after its first year of delivery. There was room for new ideas, and those who had seen their own suggestions translated into realities gave the children's spirituality proposal a favourable hearing. This project is now operational.